# BOUJEE BUBBLES

*Ashley Buonarroti*

Boujee Bubbles

Copyright © 2022 by Ashley Buonarroti

# TABLE
# OF
# CONTENTS

Welcome

WELCOME TO THE
CHAMPAGNE LIFE

4

Eight years ago, I had a fleeting vision of a Champagne lifestyle. It was a wish and an escape from my present life. I dreamed of getting to travel and drink Champagne while knowing *all* about Champagne. I dreamed of being sophisticated and feeling like I had more of a purpose than to settle for a boring life I hated.

*So this is about a journey.*

A journey of manifestation, dismantling limiting beliefs and rewriting my story exactly how I chose. I chose to rewrite the story from constant reels of getting no where, loss and victim circumstances to one where I realize I have complete control. A story where I dreamt up what I wanted, showed up that way consistently and magically, has become a reality.

5

This is about a journey.

A journey of manifestation, dismantling limiting beliefs and rewriting my story exactly how I chose to.

Several years went by and I knew I wanted out of the dead end, hamster wheel road of settling. But the vision actually lingered and became a nagging, tell tale heart kind of feeling. *Except* I wasn't doing anything about it. It seemed like a far off fantasy, shrouded by clouds, mystery and an infinite distance.

And that inner voice said to me...

'you don't come from money, you can't do that, you are not sophisticated enough, you don't know the right people, who do you think you are and so on'.

But I have loved wine since I was old enough to drink it. In fact, I took a wine cruise when I was 21. I traveled up the Napa river and visited wineries and sparkling wine houses. I was decades younger than the average person on this cruise but it cultivated my interest in wine.

I went home with new winemaking knowledge and a greater appreciation for Italian and sparkling wine.

Almost a decade later, I moved to Oregon and realized what a special gem it is in the wine world. So I became a member of a wine club that I called my *happy place*. It has beautiful gardens with water features and intimate places to sit and enjoy the peace. And a tasting room right out of Tuscany, cavelike and cozy. I mean, WOW! They hosted beautiful parties and music nights out in the garden.

I would visit every so often and ended up taking all my friends and family to visit at some point.

And then the most fitting event happened...

I lost my corporate, dead end job when they were bought out by another company.

I panicked. So in rearranging my budget, I called the winery and asked to pause my membership. The woman on the phone assured me that it was no problem and then asked me if there was anything else she could do...

I asked, 'Are you hiring?'

She said, 'Send me your resumé.'

So I did. I went to an interview the next week and was hired on the spot!

What?? Now I get to work at my happy place *and* drink fabulous wine every day?

Umm, yes. That became my reality. And it was as magical as I imagined.

Then I stumbled upon a beautiful pin on Pinterest. A sort of Champagne cart out of Australia. It was a mobile cart available for weddings and events. And that's all it took for my creative side to kick in and suddenly I had brainstormed an entire business plan. Busting at the seams, I instantly sent the picture to my sister and told her this is what we needed to do.

Still the tell tale heart was beating, urging me to open the door and peek in on that Champagne life. So I ventured out of my happy place and looked into having my very own Champagne cart. I pulled up the dusty business plan in my head and got to work.

I ordered a cart, bar supplies, registered for festivals and created a name and designed marketing materials. I got to work drinking all the Champagne, sparkling wine and sparkling wine cocktails I could get my hands on. I spent months testing my own recipes, pairing with food and delighting in the creativity I found.

Then reality kicked in. Oregon is known for long, lovely summers that sometimes spill over to October. But after that, it is a seemingly endless, gray raininess that sometimes lasts until the next July. And who wants to sit and enjoy Champagne outside in the cold rain? Certainly not me.

But as the Universe certainly wanted to let me peek in on that Champagne life, the title of Owner of a Champagne and Dessert Bar quickly landed in my lap. And it has truly been a vessel to create and share my love of Bubbly with the world.

Our small city has plenty of wineries and craft brewpubs but not a location that is elegant and bougie, centered around being able to celebrate with Champagne and Champagne cocktails.

I'm still in the pinch me phase of having a Champagne life and still defining what I want it to be.

-But I will tell you that I get to drink Champagne and Champagne cocktails as often as I'd like.

-I have weekly tastings with professionals.

-I get to attend industry exclusive events and taste the 'greats'.

-I attended the Veuve Clicquot Polo Classic in Los Angeles in 2021.

-And I get to make these beautiful cocktails for our guests every day!

So this book is dedicated to YOU- my reader. I hope to educate you, inspire you and provide you with elegant cocktails to enjoy for yourself or delight with your own guests!

Cheers!

# Intro

# INTRODUCTION TO SPARKLING WINE

I have a confession.

None of my cocktails use actual Champagne...

**I can hear the gasps now.**

And here's why-

I *do* use a sparkling wine from France but it is not Champagne. I feel for the experience and the cost of Champagne, it should be enjoyed on its own.

As a business, I can get a bottle of Champagne for $38, maybe $36 if there's a special. But most of them are $40 or more. I could probably make up that cost in the amount I sell our cocktails but would probably break even with the other ingredients, labor etc. Instead, I use an economical sparkling wine that is enjoyable on its own and complements my cocktails perfectly.

15

# DID YOU KNOW?

Not all wine with bubbles is called Champagne. In order to be labeled as Champagne, it has to be produced in the Champagne region of France. And it can only include the following grape varietals:
Chardonnay, Pinot Noir and Pinot Meunier.

So Cava for instance, is produced in Spain using the same techniques but it is outside of Champagne and other grapes are used such as:
Macabeo, Xarel-lo and Parellada.

Other sparkling wines may have a regional name such as Prosecco, Sekt, Crémant or Cava. If the wine is made in the Champagne style, look for *Traditional Method* or *Méthode Champenoise* on the label.

## Notable Champagne Producers

Roederer, Champagne house of Cristal
Taittinger
Moët & Chandon
Veuve Clicquot
Dom Perignon
Nicolas Feuillatte
GH Mumm
Laurent-Perrier
Piper-Heidsieck


## Notable Sparkling Wine Producers

Scharffenberger
Domaine Carneros
Schramsberg
Argyle
Treveri

## More Names for Sparkling Wine

Cava
Prosecco
Lambrusco
Sekt
Crémant
Moscato d'Asti

## Examples of Other Grapes Used

Xarel-lo
Muscat
Chenin Blanc
Riesling
Glera
Semillon
Lambrusco

# LET'S TALK ABOUT SWEETNESS, A.K.A. DOSAGE

There are seven different degrees of sweetness for Champagne. Champagne varietals are grown in a cooler climate and have a higher acidity when picked. 'Dosage' is the winemaker's way of balancing the acidity to round out the taste. It's also a way of adding residual sugar (RS) to sparkling wines if a certain level of sweetness is to be achieved. You'll find these listed on the label.

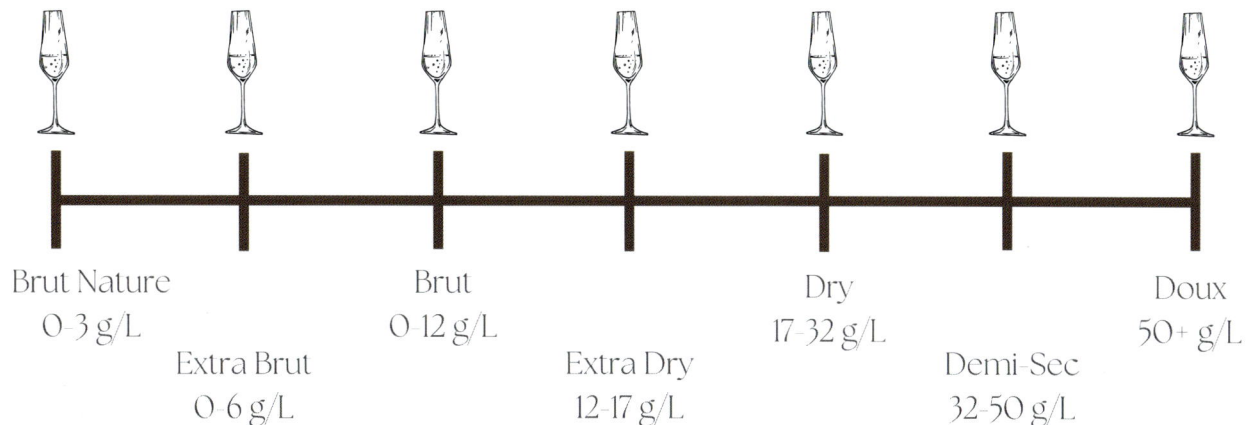

| Brut Nature | Extra Brut | Brut | Extra Dry | Dry | Demi-Sec | Doux |
|---|---|---|---|---|---|---|
| 0-3 g/L | 0-6 g/L | 0-12 g/L | 12-17 g/L | 17-32 g/L | 32-50 g/L | 50+ g/L |

The most common level of sweetness is Brut. So when you see Brut on the ingredient list for the recipes, you'll want to look for that on the label. Many recipes have fruit juices or simple syrups so I like to balance it out with a drier, sparkling wine.

A couple of notes about sweetness

When pairing sparkling wine or Champagne with desserts, such as cake at a wedding, you'll want to pair it with something a little sweeter. The higher level of acidity in a Brut does not complement the sweetness of the dessert. So it will taste bitter, instead of decadently,sweet.

As for Prosecco, I want to set the myth straight about it being sweet. Prosecco is not traditionally sweet. If a Prosecco is sweet, RS is added to supplement the taste because the quality is on the poorer side. No judgment if sweet Prosecco is your jam!

# Glassware

## THE IMPORTANCE OF THE RIGHT GLASSWARE

# A GUIDE TO GLASSWARE

I'm a sucker for novelty. I think it adds to the experience. I think a cocktail should have the appropriate or most fitting style of glassware.

I mean, who wants to drink Champagne out of a pint glass? By the time you finish, it would be warm and flat. And no, that's not a challenge. A delicate flute or coupe glass is just as easy to refill as a pint glass.

Glass makers have painstakingly put research and science into their designs based on the drink's qualities.

23

For instance, a Burgundy goblet is designed to have an expansive, round bowl. Some of them even have a bit of a lip on them for the wine to flow over your palette since Pinot Noir wine is known for its aromatics. Plus, you want the large bowl for swirling and to allow the aromas to open up. When you swirl, the taste and smell varies greatly from your first sip.

Consequently, you wouldn't serve a port in a Burgundy wine glass. It's fortified with a higher alcohol content and sugar level so it doesn't need to be swirled. Instead, sipped.

So I encourage you to invest in proper glassware for your favorite cocktails.

For our purposes, we are using glassware based on tradition, novelty or the best utility of the glass for the cocktail. Most cocktails are served in a coupe glass because I have a strong draw to their elegance, which makes them so pretty.

At the Champagne Bar I can bet money, depending on the demographic of the customer, who will be taking a photo of the cocktail as soon as it hits the table! I rarely lose and honestly that's what I strive for. I want an elegant and pretty experience with the presentation.

Use the photo as a reference but don't feel the need to go out and buy every type all at once. Take a look at the cocktails you will make most and start there.

# GLASSWARE

**Previous page (clockwise):**

Champagne flute, coupe glass, Mason Jar, rocks glass, copper mug, pint glass.

**This page (from back left, clockwise):**

Pint glass, decorative coupe glass, tumbler or stemless wine glass, rocks glass.

28

# TOOLS

WHY TOOLS
MATTER

# COCKTAIL TOOLS

Like glassware, bar tools have a place and utility to them. Take a look at the recipes you will make often and purchase your tool selection from there.

If you have to build from scratch, I recommend starting with:

*pour spouts
*jigger
*cocktail shaker
*strainer
*Y peeler

31

# From top, then L to R clockwise:

1. Mixing Spoon- use with the mixing glass.

2. Channel Peeler/Zester-the smaller holes are perfect for dragging through a citrus skin to get small zests of the skin while the channel allows you to pull through a thicker cut for twists.

3. Vegetable peeler-used for making the carrot garnish.

4. Y peeler- I love the Y peeler. The shape makes it easy to hold while peeling the outer layer of citrus for a garnish without pulling out the pith. Easier, safer and more consistent than using a paring knife.

5. Cocktail strainer-strains out the liquid you want for the cocktail.

6. Jigger-there are different sizes but a handy tool to measure ounces of liquid when making a cocktail.

7. Pour spout- put in place of the liquor bottle lid. This allows for more controlled pours into a jigger or cocktail shaker.

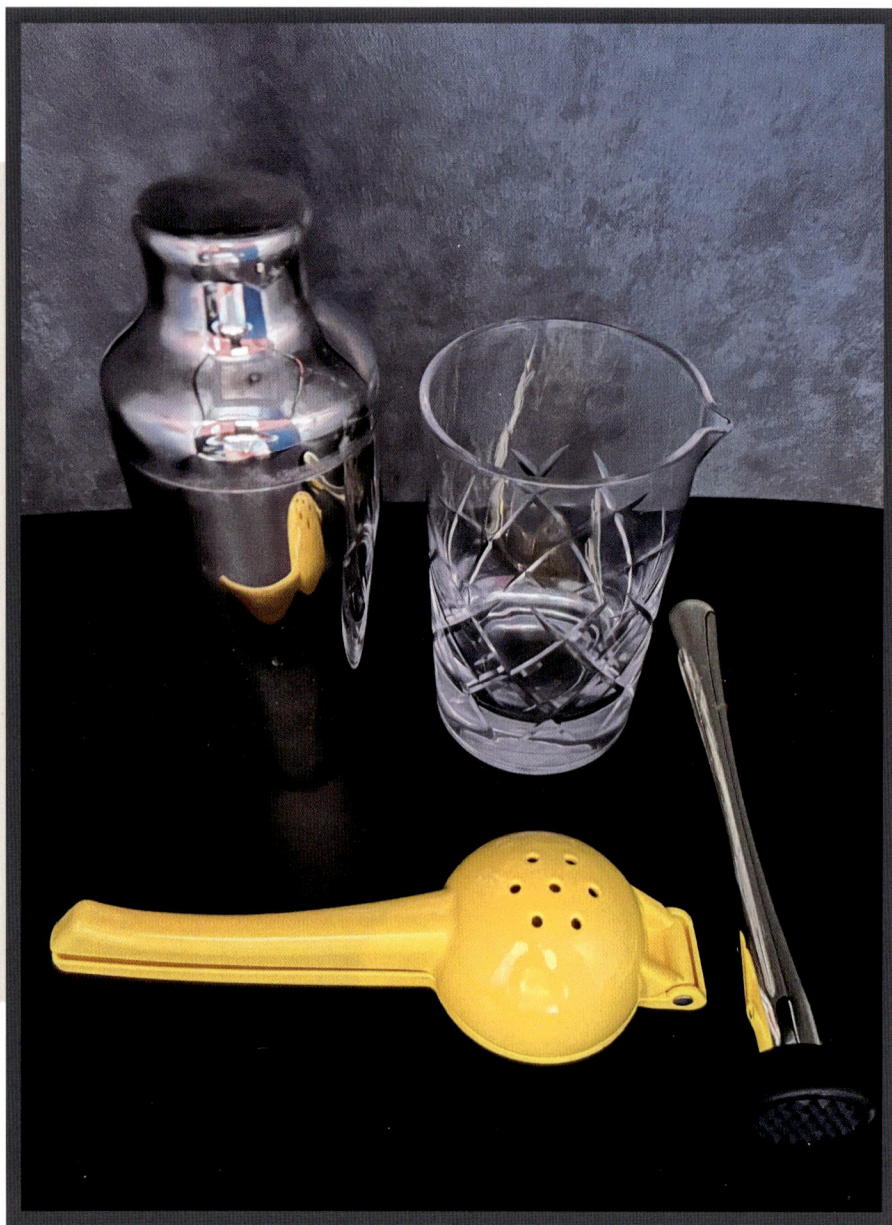

# Clockwise:

8. Cocktail Shaker- used with ice, this not only cools down your liquids but blends the flavors together. It's perfect for when egg whites or simple syrups are used.

9. Mixing glass-this has a wider base to allow for better stirring than a cocktail shaker.

10. Muddler-use to press lightly to release oils, aromatics and flavors from fruits or herbs.

11. Juicer-Best for citrus, this presses the juice out so there's no hassle with seeds.

12. (not pictured) Mandoline-for firmer pieces of produce such as a golden beet or purple sweet potato. It is efficient and safe at creating consistently thin slices.

# Garnishes

ADDING

ZHUZH

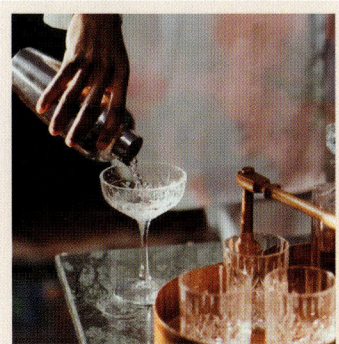

As the title mentions, we are going to add some zhuzh to our cocktails with our garnishes. We could have the most delicious cocktails in hand and your taste buds would appreciate the balance and smoothness. But we want to glam it up to have a jaw dropping experience. I want you to be wowed. I want you to be able to wow your guests.

I have given you some beginner level garnishes to zhuzh up your cocktails in a major way. Using the items from the tools section and directions from the recipes, you'll be well on your way to having your guests take pictures of your cocktails.

Not listed are how to make dehydrated lemon peels, candied pear slices or fruit caviar. Those you can purchase or easily make on your own.

# GARNISHES

## CLOCKWISE FROM TOP LEFT CORNER:

-Citrus Peel
-Citrus coin (can be used with carrot too)
-Wedge
-Citrus twist

# GARNISHES

## CLOCKWISE FROM TOP LEFT CORNER:

-Dehydrated sweet potato w/mango caviar
-Blueberries with lemon peel scroll
-Orange slice pumpkin
-Lemon peel with half a strawberry
-Golden Beet rosette

# RIBBONS
# &
# SCROLLS

From top clockwise:

-Double Bubble gum ribbon
-peeled carrot ribbon with mint
-lemon peel pierced to a scroll, or heart shape

42

# Syrups & Infusions

## SIMPLE, ELEGANT & FULL OF FLAVOR

## SIMPLE SYRUP

½ c. sugar
½ c. water

This recipe can be amended to make larger batches depending on the usage. Just keep a 1:1 ratio.

Warm water over medium heat in a small saucepan and add sugar. Stir until it dissolves. Remove from heat and allow to cool. Store in an airtight container and place in the fridge. When stored properly, this will keep for 30 days. Lots of cocktails to be made!

## Boozy strawberry simple syrup
-½ c. chopped strawberries
-½ c. rosé or sparkling rosé wine
-½ c. water
-1 c. sugar

## Vanilla simple syrup
-1 c. sugar
-1 c. water
-1 Tbs. vanilla extract

This is the same concept of the simple syrup recipe. We're just adding two more ingredients. We want a true strawberry flavor and color so strawberries are added to the mix with the sugar. I like to add the rosé for the aromatics.

Follow the recipe for the simple syrup and add the rosé and strawberries with the sugar. Cook until sugar is dissolved. Then turn off the heat but leave for at least 20 minutes until the desired color is reached. Stir often to incorporate the flavor & color. When ready to store, strain into a container and store in the refrigerator.

For the vanilla simple syrup, warm water over medium heat in a small saucepan and add sugar and vanilla. Stir until it dissolves. Remove from heat and allow to cool. Store in an airtight container and place in the fridge. When stored properly, this will keep for 30 days.

## Ube simple syrup
1 Tbs. Ube paste
¼ c. light rum
¼ c. water
½ c. sugar

Another boozy simple syrup to add to your repertoire. (If you want to omit the rum, replace it with water for a total ½ c. water.)

Warm water over medium heat in a small saucepan and add rum, paste and sugar. Heat until a low boil and simmer for 5 minutes. This burns off some of the alcohol in the rum while retaining the flavor. Let cool then refrigerate in an airtight container.

## Cinnamon Simple Syrup
2 cinnamon sticks
½ c. water
½ c. sugar

Warm water over medium heat in a small saucepan and add sugar and cinnamon sticks. Bring to a low boil and simmer for 5 minutes. Turn off heat and let the mixture steep for 4-6 hours. Remove sticks from the syrup and refrigerate in an airtight container.

## Butterfly tea simple syrup

¼ c. butterfly pea flower tea
½ c. sugar
½ c. water

Warm water over medium heat in a small saucepan and add sugar and tea. Stir until the sugar dissolves. Turn off heat. Let tea steep for 20-30 minutes, stirring occasionally. When desired color is reached, strain into an airtight container and refrigerate.

48

## Spiced Orange Simple Syrup

Peels from an orange
1 cinnamon stick
1 star anise
1 tsp. vanilla extract
½ c. water
½ c. sugar

With your Y peeler, peel off ½ skin of an orange. Warm water over medium heat in a small saucepan. Add the remaining ingredients. Bring to a low boil and simmer for 5 minutes. Turn off heat and let the mixture steep for 1-2 hours. Strain liquid and refrigerate in an airtight container.

## Rose infused gin
2 c. gin
2 roses pulled from the stem

Separate rose petals individually and place in a sealable container of gin. Infuse for 24+ hours. When ready to use, strain rose petals and place the gin in the refrigerator.

## Turmeric infused vodka
750 ml vodka
½ lb. turmeric root, peeled and chopped

Place peeled & chopped turmeric in a quart jar. Cover with vodka. Cover with lid. Infuse for 3 days or until desired color is reached. When ready to use, remove turmeric and refrigerate.

## Candy cane vodka
750 ml bottle of vodka
6 full size candy canes crushed

Add crushed candy canes to a large jar. Pour over vodka and shake. Let sit 24 hours, shaking occasionally. Strain vodka and refrigerate in a sealed container.

49

## Watermelon simple syrup
1 lb. cubed watermelon
1 c. sugar

In a gallon sized baggie, add watermelon and pour over sugar. Seal bag and lightly squeeze watermelon, mixing the two ingredients. Store in the refrigerator for 24 hours. This is a fantastic way to get a simple syrup without any cooking or cooling. As you guessed it, watermelon is made up of mostly water so it just needs to sit there and macerate for a while. After 24 hours, strain liquid out and refrigerate in an airtight container.

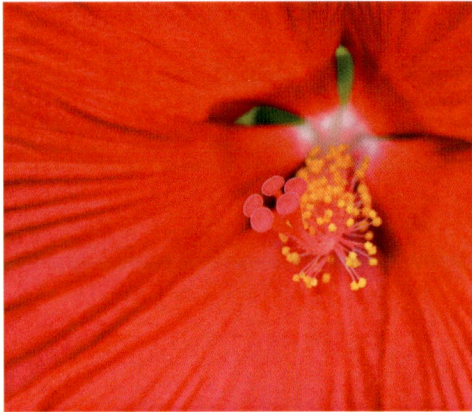

## Hibiscus Simple Syrup
¼ c. dried hibiscus flowers
½ c. water
½ c. sugar

In a small saucepan, warm water over medium heat. Add hibiscus flowers and sugar. Bring to a low boil and simmer for 5 minutes. Turn off heat and let the mixture steep for 1-2 hours. In a strainer, strain out liquid from flowers. Allow to cool and refrigerate in an airtight container.

50

## Pear Tea Simple Syrup
1 pear tea bag contents or ¼ c. loose leaf pear tea
½ bosc pear chopped
½ c. water
½ c. sugar

Warm water over medium heat in a small saucepan and add tea, pears and sugar. Bring to a low boil and simmer for 5 minutes. Turn off heat and let the mixture steep for 1-2 hours. In a strainer, strain out liquid. Allow to cool and refrigerate in an airtight container.

# cocktails

CHAMPAGNE
COCKTAILS

In the summer of 2021, I found myself with more time on my hands. So I started experimenting. I made my first frosé and Aperol Spritz. I had ordered these before but never made my own.

I expanded my food and wine pairing knowledge to cocktails, wanting to enhance a meal. Or let's be honest, it had to be delicious *and* look incredible.

So I wrote what I consider the OG cocktail list. These are the cocktails that were the foundation for my business and have been a hit ever since. Starting with the *Tiffany Who* to the *Mistletoe Martini*.

With the creation of these cocktails, I have been inspired by classics but many of them are attributed to men, such as the Boulevardier. I created my own version but decided to call it Boulevardiva.

And I will pay tribute to Anders Erickson's Mai Tai. His creation truly inspired the Mai Doll. Every woman needs a Mai Doll from time to time.

## Classic
2 oz. orange juice
4 oz. Brut
Orange wedge

Pour orange juice into a flute. Top with Brut.
Garnish rim with orange wedge.

## Carrot
1.5 oz. carrot juice
.5 oz. spiced orange syrup
.25 oz. ginger liqueur
4 oz. Brut
Orange wedge

Pour juice, syrup and liqueur into a mixing glass and stir. Top with Brut. Garnish with orange wedge.

## Apple Cider
2 oz. apple cider
4 oz. Brut
1 tsp. cinnamon
1 Tbs. sugar
Apple slice or apple cinnamon donut, for garnish

Mix cinnamon and sugar. Rim edge of glass. Pour cider into a flute. Top with Brut. Garnish rim with apple slice or donut.

*Mimosas*

## Cranberry
¼ c. cranberry juice
5 oz. Brut
2 whole cranberries
Rosemary sprig
lime wedge or juice, for rim
sugar, for rim

Rim a champagne flute with lime juice then dip in sugar. Add cranberry juice and top with Brut. Use a toothpick to bore a hole in the center of both cranberries. Then thread the hole with the rosemary sprig. Serve on top of rim.

54

## Pumpkin base
1 can pumpkin purée (15 oz. can)
1 tbsp pumpkin pie spice
3 tbsp sugar
1 cup water

## For the mimosa
1.5 oz. pumpkin base
5 oz. sparkling wine
canned whip cream
cinnamon stick
1 Tbs. pumpkin pie spice, for rim
1/2 c. sugar, for rim

To make the juice, add all the ingredients of the base to a small saucepan. Heat over medium until warm and all flavors are blended, stirring frequently.

Remove from heat and strain through a fine mesh sieve. It should still be a purée that is not too thick. Discard remaining purée and completely cool in the refrigerator.

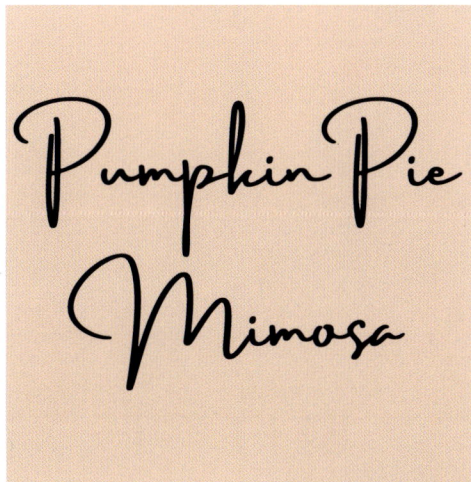

*Pumpkin Pie Mimosa*

Mix ingredients for the rim. This is a large batch and can be stored. To rim, wet the rim of the glass with lemon juice then dip into the sugar mixture.

Pour 1.5-2 oz. of pumpkin mixture into a flute. Top with sparkling wine. Then garnish with a fluff of whip cream and a cinnamon stick. Sprinkle with pinch of the rimming sugar.

55

# BELLINI

2 oz. unsweetened peach purée
5 oz. Prosecco
Peach slice for garnish

Add the purée to a flute and top with Prosecco. Garnish with
a fresh peach slice.

# TIFFANY WHO?

1 oz. Blue Curaçao
2 oz. lemonade
2 oz. Brut
silver sprinkles

Rim flute with lemon juice then dip in silver sugar. Pour Blue Curaçao and lemonade in shaker w/ice. Shake for 10-15 seconds. Strain into flute. Top with Brut.

# IT'S WHITNEY BITCH

1.5 oz. Pink Whitney vodka
1 oz. strawberry simple syrup
1 oz. lemon juice
2 oz. Prosecco rosé
strawberry quarter
lemon peel strip

Yep, I said it. I bet you did too!

This is by far the most popular cocktail in our Champagne Bar. I'm pretty sure it's 50% the novelty of the name and 50%, it's just that good!

Add ice to cocktail shaker. Pour vodka, syrup and lemon juice in shaker w/ice. Shake. Strain into coupe glass and top w/Prosecco. Add garnish from page 40.

# MAPLE SOUR

1.5 oz. Pisco
1 oz. maple syrup
1 oz. lemon juice
Pinch of freshly ground pink salt
1 egg white
2 oz. Brut
Angostura bitters
Mound of maple cotton candy

In a cocktail shaker filled with ice, add Pisco, syrup, juice, salt and egg white. Shake vigorously 20-30 seconds until frothy. Strain into coupe glass. Delicately top with Brut in one location so the foam is not disrupted. Top with several drops of bitters. Pierce a small mound of cotton candy and serve separately or on the side of the glass.

# SASSY

1.5 oz. Ancho Reyes Verde
1 oz. guava purée
1 oz. pineapple juice
1.5 oz. Brut

Lime juice
Freshly ground salt
Espelette
pineapple wedge
4 jalapeño coins

Mix equal parts salt and espelette for rim. Coat the rim with lime juice, then dip in salt/espelette mix. Add ice to mason jar. Add cocktail ingredients to shaker. Shake. Strain liquid into jar. Add two jalapeño coins. Top with Brut. Garnish rim with pineapple wedge and remaining jalepeño coins.

60

# DOUBLE BUBBLE TROUBLE

1.5 oz. vanilla vodka

1 oz. bubble gum syrup

1/2 oz. lemon juice

1.5 oz. rosé Prosecco

6 inch Double Bubble gum strip

Add vodka, syrup and lemon juice to a cocktail shaker with ice. Shake for 10-15 seconds. Strain into coupe glass. Top with rosé Prosecco. Weave bubble gum strip onto cocktail pick.

# MAI DOLL

EVERY WOMAN NEEDS A MAI DOLL NOW AND THEN

# MAI DOLL

1 oz. light rum
.5 oz. dark rum
.5 oz. orange curaçao
Freshly squeezed juice of 1/2 lime
.5 oz. orgeat syrup
Brut
cocktail cherry
1/2 of lime as a bowl (squeezed)
rum 151
hefty sprig of mint

Fill a plastic bag or Lewis bag with a cup of ice. Smash it with a meat or wooden mallet. Pour into cocktail shaker. Add all cocktail ingredients to shaker except Brut and shake for 15-20 seconds. Pour all into a mason jar. Top with Brut. Invert the lime into a little bowl. Add a cocktail cherry and place on top of the beverage. Take the mint and place between the glass and the lime bowl. Add a small amount of the 151 Rum to the 'bowl' and light on fire.
Make sure you blow it out before you drink it!

63

# ORANGE CREAMSICLE POPTAIL

Place the creamsicle in a coupe glass. In a cocktail shaker filled with ice, add orange juice, half and half and vodka. Shake for 10-15 seconds until nice and frothy. Strain into glass around the creamsicle. Top with Brut. Then grate fresh orange zest over.

1 creamsicle
¼ c. orange juice
½ oz. half and half
1 oz. vanilla vodka
1.5 oz. Brut
Orange zest

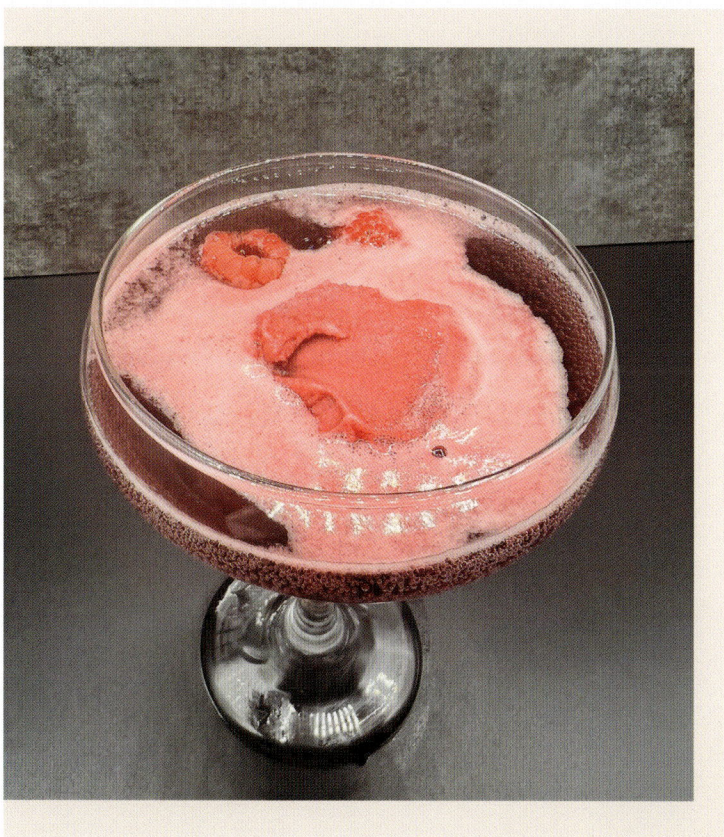

# RASPBERRY SGROPPINO

1 scoop raspberry sorbet
1 oz. Chambord
1.5 oz. Brut
.5 oz. triple sec
2 fresh raspberries

Place the scoop of raspberry sorbet in a coupe glass. Swirl and top with Chambord and triple sec. Lightly stir. Add Brut. Garnish with fresh raspberries.

# ARNOLD PALMER POPTAIL

Place popsicle in coupe glass. Add limoncello and top with Brut. Add a lemon twist to the rim or on top of the liquid.

- Sweet tea popsicle
- 1 oz. limoncello from freezer
- 3 oz. Brut
- Lemon twist for garnish

# PEACHY KEEN POPTAIL

PEACH POPSICLE
1 OZ. WHIPPED VODKA
1/2 OZ. PEACH SCHNAPPS
1/2 OZ. PEACH PURÉE
1.5 OZ. BRUT

ADD LIQUIDS TO SHAKER WITH ICE.
STRAIN INTO COUPE GLASS.
TOP WITH BRUT AND PEACH POPSICLE.

# LAVENDER LEMON DROP SPRITZ

1.5 OZ. LAVENDER VODKA
2 PUMPS LAVENDER SYRUP
1.5 OZ. LEMON JUICE
2 OZ. BRUT
LEMON TWIST
LAVENDER SPRIG

ADD ICE TO A COCKTAIL SHAKER.
ADD VODKA, SYRUP AND JUICE AND SHAKE FOR 10-15 SECONDS.
STRAIN AND POUR INTO COUPE GLASS. TOP WITH BRUT.
GARNISH RIM WITH DRIED LEMON AND LAVENDER SPRIG, (OPTIONAL).

68

# PUMPKIN SPICE SPLASH

## For the cocktail:
1 oz. pumpkin purée
1/2 oz. honey
Juice squeezed from 1/2 a lime
1 oz. vodka
2 oz. ginger beer
1.5 oz Brut

## For the garnish:
1 orange slice, peel removed

lime peel cut with paring knife to look like pumpkin stem

This could be a pumpkin mule but I prefer to call it a splash with the Brut and the fact that I serve it in a rocks glass. You can use a copper mule cup if you like.

In a cocktail shaker, add ice, purée, honey, lime juice and vodka. Shake for 10-15 seconds. Add ice to rocks glass. Strain mixture into glass. Add ginger beer and Brut. For garnish, place lime 'stem' in the middle of the orange slice and place on top.

69

# POISONED POMME

Taking the French word for apple and using it to describe apple & pomegranate adds to the character of this fun, fall cocktail!

1 oz. vodka
2 oz. apple pomegranate juice
1/2 lime, squeezed
1.5 oz. Brut
gold sanding sugar

In a cocktail shaker, add vodka and juices. Shake 10-15 seconds. Rim tumbler glass (or stemless wine glass) with gold sugar. Add ice. Strain into glass. Serve immediately.

# FIZZY PEARFECTION

1.5 oz. vodka
2 oz. pear juice
.5 oz. lemon juice
1.5 oz. Brut
candied pear slice
cinnamon stick, sprig of
rosemary

In a cocktail shaker, add
vodka and juices. Shake
10-15 seconds. Strain into
coupe glass. Top with
Brut. Garnish with candied
pear, cinnamon stick and
rosemary sprig.
Cinnamon stick can be lit
on fire for more
aromatics for the fall
season.

# NIGHTMARE ON MADISON STREET

1/4 c. cherry juice
1/2 oz. Cognac
1 sugar cube
4-6 drops Angostura bitters
5 oz. Brut

2 whole lychees
2 black olives
red food coloring

This is a Halloween version of a Champagne cocktail. It definitely sparks conversation amongst guests!

Add sugar cube to a coupe glass. Add 5-6 drops of bitters. Pour Cognac over sugar cube. Top with sparkling wine.

For the lychee eyeballs, place an olive inside a lychee and repeat for the second eye. Pierce with a cocktail pick to stabilize. Take a toothpick and dip into red food coloring and dot the tops of the lychee. The liquid will make the dye expand and look bloodshot. A little goes a long way and you might want to wear gloves!

# FULL MOONTINI

1.5 oz. light rum
1 oz. pineapple juice
Juice from 1/2 lime
1/8 tsp. activated charcoal
(food grade)
1.5 oz. Brut

In a cocktail shaker, add rum, juices and charcoal. Shake vigorously for 10-15 seconds. Place large ice sphere into coupe glass. Strain into glass. Top with Brut.

# CANDY CANE LANE

1 oz. candy cane vodka
1 oz. crème de cacao (clear)
½ oz. vanilla simple syrup
1.5 oz. rosé Prosecco
Mini candy cane
Crushed candy cane for rim

Add vodka, crème de cacao and simple syrup to a cocktail shaker. Shake for 10-15 seconds. Rim coupe glass with simple syrup and crushed candy cane. Strain liquid into coupe glass. Top with Brut and add a mini candy cane as a garnish.

# MISTLETOE MARTINI

1.5 oz. vodka

½ oz. elderflower liqueur

2 oz. cranberry juice

½ oz. simple syrup

1.5 oz. Brut

Cranberries & rosemary sprig for garnish

Add vodka, liqueur, juice and simple syrup to a cocktail shaker and shake for 10-15 seconds. Strain into a coupe glass and top with Brut. Garnish with cranberries and a sprig of rosemary.

# THE PRINCESS
# AND
# THE PEA

1 oz. butterfly tea simple syrup
1 oz. vanilla vodka
3 oz. Brut
lemon peel strip, formed into a
scroll (pg. 40)
2 blueberries

Pour simple syrup into coupe
glass. Add vodka. Stir. Top with
Brut.

Pierce one blueberry, add
scroll, finish with one more
blueberry on the end and
place over glass rim.

# CHAMPAGNE MARGARITA

1.5 oz. tequila
.5 oz. triple sec
½ lime, squeezed
3 oz. Brut
1 lime wedge for garnish
salt for rim

Rim the edge of a rocks glass with lime juice and dip in salt. In a cocktail shaker, add tequila, triple sec and lime juice to ice. Shake for 10-15 seconds. Pour contents into glass and top with Brut. Garnish with lime wedge.

# SORRENTO PEAR SPRITZ

1 oz. vodka
.75 oz. limoncello
.75 oz. ginger liqueur
.5 oz. pear simple syrup
2 oz. orange juice
1 oz. Brut
pear slices
mint sprig

Add crushed ice to a cocktail shaker then add vodka, limoncello, ginger liqueur, simple syrup and juice. Shake. Pour into a Collins glass. Top with more ice. Add Brut. Garnish with the mint & pear.

# DESERT SUN ELIXIR

-1.5 oz. tequila
-1.5 oz. grapefruit juice
-1/2 oz. cinnamon syrup
-1/4 oz. turmeric tea
-2 oz. Brut
-Grapefruit slice

Fill a cocktail shaker and rocks glass with ice. Add tequila, grapefruit juice, syrup and tea to the shaker. Shake 10-15 seconds. Strain and pour over ice in glass. Top with Brut and garnish with a grapefruit slice. Can be brûléed with sugar and a torch as in picture.

# HIBISCUS PALOMA

1.5 oz. tequila
.75 oz. hibiscus syrup
.5 oz lime juice
2 oz. grapefruit juice
2 oz. sparkling wine
1 tsp each of salt & sugar
1 tsp ground hibiscus tea (from teabag)

Take a coupe glass and dip the rim in lime juice and then the hibiscus tea mixture. Add ice to a cocktail shaker. Add tequila, syrup, and juices. Shake for 10-15 seconds. Strain and pour into the rimmed coupe glass. Top with sparkling wine.

# CARDAMOM ROSE FIZZ

2 oz. rose infused Gin
1.5 oz. grapefruit juice
.5 oz. lemon juice
.5 oz. simple syrup
1 cardamom pod
2 dashes rose water
1 oz. Brut
Golden Beet rose garnish

Add ice to a rocks glass. In a shaker
cup, lightly muddle cardamom pod
by cracking open the pod. Add gin,
juices and simple syrup with ice.
Shake well. Strain into glass. Add Brut
and spritz with rose water. Garnish
with premade Golden Beet rose.

# LIFE OF THE PEAR-TY

1 oz. green chartreuse liqueur
.5 oz. pear tea simple syrup
Squeeze of ½ lemon
4 oz. Brut
lemon slice

In a mixing glass, add ice, liqueur, simple syrup and lemon juice. Stir for at least 30 seconds. Strain into a coupe glass. Top with Brut. Then add a lemon twist on top for the garnish.

# BOULEVARDIVA

1.5 oz. Bourbon
.5 oz. sweet Vermouth
.5 oz. Campari
.25 oz. Nocino
Brut
Orange peel coin

Add ice to a rocks glass.
Add Bourbon, Vermouth,
Campari and Nocino.

Stir for at least 30
seconds. Top with Brut.
Garnish with an orange
peel coin.

# TURMERIC SPLASH

1.5 oz. turmeric vodka
1 oz. carrot juice
.5 oz. lemon juice
.5 oz. honey
2 dashes celery bitters
1.5 oz. Brut
carrot ribbon

Fill a Collins glass with ice. Add all ingredients except Brut to a cocktail shaker. Shake for 15-20 seconds. Strain into glass over ice. Top with Brut. Garnish with carrot ribbon.

# STRAWBERRY BASIL SMASH

1.5 oz. gin
3 strawberries, chopped
½ strawberry for garnish
2 basil leaves
.5 oz. lime juice
1 oz. simple syrup
3 oz. Brut

Add berries and basil to a cocktail shaker and muddle together. Add ice to a mason jar. Scoop out the berry mixture and spoon into the glass. Add ice, gin, lime juice and simple syrup to the cocktail shaker and shake for 10-15 seconds. Strain into the glass. Top with Brut and garnish with strawberry.

# WATERMELON MINT JULEP

1.5 oz. bourbon
½ oz. watermelon simple syrup
4-1 inch cubes of watermelon
4 to 6 fresh mint leaves
depending on size
1.5 oz. Brut
Fresh mint sprig and
watermelon wedge for garnish

Muddle watermelon and simple
syrup in a julep cup. Add mint and
muddle together. Add bourbon and
stir. Then add crushed ice. Stir to
mix and add more crushed ice. Top
with Brut and garnish with a mint
sprig and watermelon wedge.

# WATERMELON MOJITO

1.5 oz. light rum
½ oz. watermelon simple syrup
4-1 inch cubes of watermelon
4 large mint sprigs
½ fresh squeezed lime
1.5 oz. Brut
twisted lemon slice
2 watermelon balls (quarter sized)

Scoop fresh watermelon balls and set aside. Add rum, cubed watermelon, mint and simple syrup to cocktail shaker and lightly muddle. Add ice and shake for 10-15 seconds. Strain into a rocks glass over fresh ice. Top with Brut. Garnish with the twisted lemon slice and the two watermelon balls.

# BELLADONNA

1 PEACH HALVED AND
PITTED
1 TBS. HONEY
1 TSP. CINNAMON
1/4 C. WATER
1.5 OZ. GIN
1.5 OZ. BRUT
LARGE LEAF OF BASIL
PEACH SLICE

PREHEAT OVEN TO 420 DEGREES. PLACE PEACH SLICES ON PARCHMENT PAPER OR SILICONE MAT. DRIZZLE WITH HONEY AND SPRINKLE WITH CINNAMON. (THIS CAN EASILY BE MULTIPLIED.) ROAST FOR 20 MINUTES. REMOVE FROM THE OVEN AND PURÉE IN A BLENDER WITH WATER UNTIL SMOOTH. STRAIN THROUGH A WIRE MESH STRAINER.

ADD 1.5 OZ. PEACH PURÉE TO A COCKTAIL SHAKER. ADD ICE, GIN AND LEMON JUICE. SHAKE FOR 10-15 SECONDS. STRAIN INTO A ROCKS GLASS FILLED WITH FRESH ICE. TOP WITH BRUT AND GARNISH WITH A BASIL LEAF AND PEACH SLICE.

# CARROT COLADA

1 OZ. COCONUT RUM

1.5 OZ. COCONUT WATER

1 OZ. CARROT JUICE

1 OZ. ORANGE JUICE

2 OZ. BRUT

CARROT GARNISH

ADD RUM, COCONUT WATER AND JUICES TO A SHAKER. SHAKE AND STRAIN INTO A COUPE GLASS. TOP WITH BRUT. ADD CARROT GARNISH.

# DIS–UBE
# THE
# RULES

1.5 oz. light rum
.5 oz. Ube simple syrup
.5 oz. pineapple juice
1 egg white
2 oz. Brut
1 dried sweet potato chip
1 tsp. mango caviar


Add ice to cocktail shaker.
Measure out and add all liquids to shaker.
Shake vigorously for at least 30 seconds. (Egg whites need time to froth.)
Strain into coupe glass.
Top with Brut
Place dried sweet potato chip on the edge of the glass and half on top of the foam.
Add mango caviar on top of the sweet potato.

# CRANBERRY MULE

1.5 oz. vodka
2 oz. cranberry juice
3 oz. ginger beer
½ lime, squeezed
1.5 oz. Brut
Handful of fresh or
frozen cranberries
1 lime wedge

Fill a copper mule cup with ice. Add vodka, juices and ginger beer. Stir to mix and cool down. Top with Brut and extra ice, if desired. Toss in the handful of cranberries and lime wedge for garnish.

# GLOSSARY

---

Cava-a Spanish sparkling wine made in the same way as Champagne

Champagne-a white sparkling wine made in the Champagne region of France

Garnish-decorative element that adds character or style to a mixed drink

Infusion-technique where an ingredient is added for the flavor desired to a liquid. It is 'infused' for a period of time then removed

Muddle-method of lightly mashing fruit, herbs or spices for cocktails

Poptail-popsicle + cocktail

Prosecco-a sparkling wine made from the Veneto region of northeastern Italy

Zhuzh-make more exciting, lively or attractive

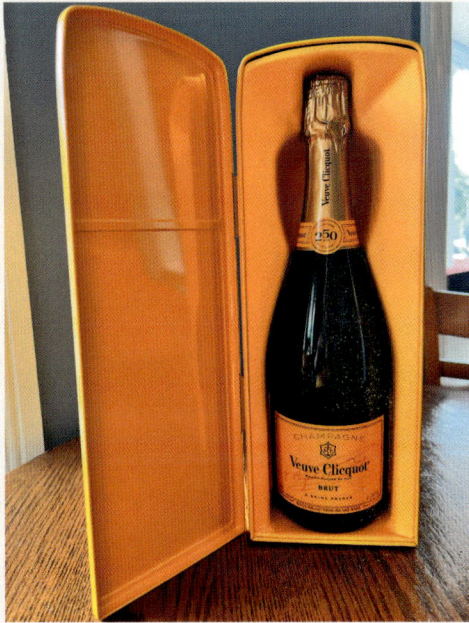